PatkauArchitects

PatkauArchitects

Introduction by Kenneth Frampton

THE MONACELLI PRESS

Library of Congress Cataloging-in-Publication Data
Patkau Architects / introduction by Kenneth Frampton.
p. cm.
ISBN 1-58093-169-3
1. Patkau Architects (Firm). 2. Architecture—Canada—
20th century. 3. Architecture—Canada—21st century.
I. Frampton, Kenneth. II. Patkau Architects (Firm).
NA749.P38P374 2006
720.92'2—dc22   2006002340

Printed and bound in China

Designed by George Vaitkunas

The architects gratefully acknowledge the support
of the Canada Council for the Arts for this publication.

Canada Council Conseil des Arts
for the Arts   du Canada

Contents

7 **Reflective Practice** Kenneth Frampton

22 **Seabird Island School**
34 **Canadian Clay and Glass Gallery**
48 **Newton Library**
56 **Barnes House**
70 **Strawberry Vale School**
92 **Shaw House**
106 **Agosta House**
118 **Nursing and Biomedical Sciences Building, University of Texas Houston Health Science Center**
126 **La Petite Maison du Weekend**
130 **Grande Bibliothèque du Québec**
164 **Gleneagles Community Centre**
176 **Winnipeg Centennial Library Addition**
188 **Centre for Music, Art, and Design, University of Manitoba**
200 **Protoype Cottage**
208 **Little House**
216 **New College House Student Residence, University of Pennsylvania**
226 **University Square, University of British Columbia**

237 Collaborators
238 Project Credits
240 Photography Credits

space is governed by an inverted pitched roof, low at the center and high on the perimeter. Located on a flat site planted with an assortment of evergreen and deciduous trees in the midst of a low-density suburb, Newton Library houses its entire program under a continuous, inverted roof, the axis of which is carried on a line of reinforced-concrete columns. These are linked longitudinally by a laminated timber beam that extends across the columns for the entire length of the building. Transverse laminated timber frames take their bearing off this spine, with each span being picked up on the perimeter by inclined laminated props that establish the outer perimeter of the building. Due to the fact that an exposed timber structure would be excessively light absorbent, the architects opted for finishing the interior, apart from the framing, in painted plasterboard in order to bounce the light off the inclined soffits. As they put it:

In the Newton Library, we started to think about the positive qualities of "skins" in architecture. This began from a concern that light at the edges of a deep floor plate would be able to penetrate a significant way into that plate. Light colored, monolithic drywall surfaces are ideal for this. We used white painted drywall to bounce light deep into section in that project.[7]

The highly sculptural quality of the exterior form of Newton derives in large measure from the mechanical attic that, cradled in the valley of the roof, progressively diminishes toward the ends of the building as the volume required for the air-conditioning ducts correspondingly decreases. This diminishment in the section is par-tially represented by the progressive delamination of the cladding. As the architects have noted:

Where its luminous and enclosing characteristics are not required the layer of cladding is feathered out to its own thickness, eventually giving way to exposed construction. This allows the tectonic, more durable parts of the building to extend outside as a rain canopy . . . These assertive shapes allow the clad construction to take on a more figurative quality which enables it to act as a more positive counterpart to the robust quality of the timber and concrete. In this way dialectic of con-struction types energizes the architectural expression of the building.[8]

Emily Carr College

Seabird Island School model, opposite

Asymmetrical in plan due to the shorter and longer spans on either side of the central spine, the interior volume of the library presents itself as barnlike space under a single roof. The inherent asymmetry is reinforced by the informal disposition of a number of closed or semi-enclosed auxiliary volumes: a circulation desk and staff offices to the north, a squarish multipurpose room in the southwest corner, a children's library and offices to the south, and a single seminar room symbolically isolated as a kind of representative prow at the head of the building. All in all, Newton shifts away from the mutual influence of Aalto and Scarpa toward an audacious tectonic ingenuity that, however unconsciously, is perhaps closer to the Norwegian master Sverre Fehn.

Strawberry Vale School, on a slightly uneven, leftover site, is surely the culmination of these roofwork pieces. It may be seen as a synthesis of concepts previously broached in Seabird Island School and Newton Library. The seminal notions that motivate the parti of this building are, first, the steel-framed servicing attic that runs down the spine of the structure like a cranked vertebrae and, second, the sixteen classrooms, organized in four pods of four classrooms each that thrust out, under low eaves, into a moss-laden, rock-strewn, microlandscape close to a canopy of native oaks. The Patkaus' 1996 description of this building makes explicit reference to the micro-communal ideas about which the entire fabric was organized:

As in our first school, the classrooms are arranged facing south, grouped into pods of four and separated by the rock rifts that penetrate the site. All classrooms have doorways opening directly onto the site, providing access to the outside teaching areas. Views are aligned in multiple directions according to diagonals passing through the school and into the peripheral landscape. Each single classroom is associated with the three adjoining classrooms through a communal interior space and with three other classrooms through an exterior space. In this way, each classroom belongs both to its pod and to a larger community, relating in some way to almost half the classrooms in the school via these in-between spaces. The classrooms and communal spaces are organized along a linear spine that provides circulation below and servicing above. The plan shifts at the rock rifts, encouraging an intimacy of social space. The services above are both accessible and visible, revealing the workings

of the building to both children and adults. The servicing void also provides for extra space wherein future technological changes may be easily accommodated.[9]

The classroom pods, articulated as separate from each other, are simultaneously unified by oversailing timber roofs that, carried on a skeleton of transverse steel beams, are partially supported by tubular steel columns resting on outriding dwarf walls in concrete. This spatial setup is interwoven with the equally fugal articulation of the aluminum and timber window frames of the classrooms themselves, which were sensitively dimensioned to relate to the scale of the children. Herein, the fixed lights in aluminum are categorically distinguished from the operable windows in wood. The result is a microcosmic work of an exceptionally inflected character, and it would be difficult to find a single school of recent date that has been orchestrated with such consummate care. Like the Newton Library and the Canadian Clay and Glass Gallery, Strawberry Vale was analyzed at its completion by a cutaway structural model that demonstrated unequivocally how the cranked spine, framed in steel, was the prime mover of the undulating continuity of the space. However, it was just the density and relatively dark tone of this constructivist assembly in steel and timber that led the architects to have second thoughts about their tendency toward overarticulated tectonic forms. As they have recently remarked:

By the time we did Strawberry Vale School, we were seriously questioning the amount of information that a totally expressive tectonic system gave. A strict expression of tectonics throughout a building seemed to make the building all about itself so much. In a school, children's drawings might well be overwhelmed by tectonic information. The value of calming skins became very real to us in that project and we began to use skins (primarily in classroom spaces) to calm space at times so that the life inside could become dominant, children's drawings didn't have to compete for attention. The architecture then became about space and light and quiet surface. Of course, in a school, quiet surface is there as a support for the incredible activity of "children" surface. We continued to realize the potential of both systems in subsequent projects and attempted to deploy them according to circumstance.[10]

The development and realization of Strawberry Vale depended on the collaboration of a tightly integrated team, which led to the entry into the partnership of Michael Cunningham as a principal and later David Shone and Peter Suter as associates. Each of these figures, later to be joined by Greg Boothroyd, would make significant contributions not only to the evolution of the school but also to many of the projects subsequently tackled by the office.

A tectonic space-form and light-reflecting surfaces are both equally evident in the Barnes house (1991–93) in Nanaimo, British Columbia, on a wooded promontory overlooking the Strait of Georgia. Situated on an exceptionally dramatic site, looking out toward the mainland of British Columbia, the house is open to the sea on one side and hemmed in by forest on the other. As a result, it was designed as a belvedere, capable of focusing one's attention at two scales, that is to say, not only on the expanse of the ocean but also on the microcosm of the ferns and moss that line the natural rock crevice that constitutes the immediate environment of the raised living volume.

One enters the house through a sculptor's studio on the lower ground floor, through a prowlike metal portico cantilevering out from the northwest corner of the building. With a guest room and bathroom discreetly located at its rear, the studio doubles as a stair hall leading, via a double-height volume, to the main living level above. Given the story-height sectional displacement between front and back, this house depends on a dramatic opposition between earthwork and roofwork, the former being carved into the landfall of the site and the latter rising as a humpbacked framework of primary and secondary timber beams that deposit their weight on three cylindrical concrete columns, only two of which pass through the full height of the house. In short, this is a typical Patkau constructivist montage of the highest sophistication, as is made clear by their description:

For the most part the shell of the house is comprised of conventional wood framing, stucco clad, on a reinforced concrete grade beam foundation. Three concrete columns rise within this volume to support a heavy timber roof structure. Floors are generally exposed concrete, either as a slab-on-grade in the lower level or as a topping on wood framing in the main level. Steel is used as a counterpoint to the monolithic concrete and

Barnes house

Strawberry Vale School, opposite

*stucco clad wood framing, as elaborated connections between concrete
and heavy timber, as railings at stairs and as a canopy over the entrance
and large window facing northwest. This canopy, which is made of 10
millimeters thick steel plate, cantilevers 3.7 meters over the openings it
shelters. Interior wall surfaces are painted gypsum board.*[11]

The crowning roof, boarded ceiling, exposed rafters, and free-
standing concrete columns with angled brackets in tubular steel that
flare out from the column heads to pick up the framing of the roof
jointly evoke as a gestalt not only the aboriginal building of the
Pacific Northwest but also the Japanese vernacular cult of the *hashira.*
In Japanese tradition, this *axis mundi,* by virtue of being the main
support for the entire roof, symbolically shelters the family covered
by its span. At the same time, as elsewhere in the Patkau practice,
metal is employed in the more anthropomorphic parts of this
house, particularly the handrails and the exposed knife-edge aluminum angles backing the timber treads of the stair. The very delicate and finely proportioned fenestration, however, is made from
wood. The prime influence in all of this detailing is once again
Carlo Scarpa, a presence already evident as an inspiration eight
years earlier in the reconstructed interior that the Patkaus designed
for the Porter/Vandenbosch house in Toronto (1985–86).

The years 1995 and 1996 were crucial for the development of
the practice, for during these years the architects received three
successive commissions that caused them to rethink the overall
approach of the office. The works in question are the Shaw house
(1995–2000), built on a narrow-fronted suburban plot overlooking
English Bay, in Vancouver; the Agosta house (1996–2000), erected
as a retirement residence for a New York couple on San Juan
Island, Washington; and finally, an unbuilt project for the Nursing
and Biomedical Sciences Building (1996) at the University of Texas
in Houston. Each of these exercises entailed a return to the
orthogonal as an overriding spatial concept together with a decisive shift away from the earthwork/roofwork theme. This move is
partially explained by the fact that whereas relatively small, single-
story programs on irregular, highly topographic sites naturally
lend themselves to the earthwork/roofwork paradigm, large, cellu-
lar, multistory programs in urban settings tended to diminish the
importance of the roof.

Porter/Vandenbosch house

The Shaw house also entailed a decisive break with the timber thematic in that the architects opted in this instance for high-quality, cast-in-place reinforced concrete. Designed for a nomadic, wealthy bachelor, the program called for a primary living space plus kitchen/dining, study, music room, and lap pool. The restricted width of the plot meant that the lap pool had to be accommodated above the side entrance to the house, while the soundproof music room was relegated to the basement. This disposition accounts for the most lyrical, if not surreal, aspect of the house, namely, the fact that one approaches the front door beneath the glass bottom of the lap pool. Thus the space of entry is not only subject to the perennial refraction of light through the surface of the water but also, on occasion, to the turbulence caused by a phantom body swimming above one's head. From this aqueous threshold, a straight flight leads directly down to the music room, while another doubles back in the opposite direction to give access to the master bedroom/bathroom suite at the top of the house. This last opens directly to a private terrace situated above the garage, which in turn gives onto the eastern end of the lap pool; from here, one may swim to another terrace overlooking the ocean.

Generous ceiling heights throughout, and above all a double height over the dining area, serve to expand the apparent size of this rather tight house. This effect is heightened by the play of zenithal light illuminating the dining space from a louvered clerestory that opens toward the west. The sitting room terminates in a prowlike space, its full-height glazing opening onto the terrace facing the sea. Since Vancouver is located in an earthquake zone, the concrete frame and floor slab had to be designed to resist lateral seismic movement. The net result is a precisely finished concrete house that in many respects recalls the work of Tadao Ando, particularly with regard to the quality of the fair-faced concrete and the generally introspective character of the work.

If the Shaw house is tightly organized within a narrow suburban site, the single-story Agosta house is cast in the form of a low fence deliberately stretched out across the width of a large clearing amid a dense, second-growth forest of fir trees. Approached through a wild meadow, this louvered timber elevation permits enticing glimpses of the kitchen forecourt, along with the multiple inclined planes that comprise the body of the house, not to mention a hint of a panoramic view lying beyond. In this way, the forecourt, designed to exclude deer, initiates a series of similarly layered transverse planes and spaces. The resulting spatial sequence leads to the master bedroom on one side of the entry and to the living room on the other. The living/dining space is unified by a canted roof that continues out over a belvedere terrace. Apart from its well-serviced domesticity, one may also construe the Agosta house as a neo-constructivist light modulator in timber relief that also happens to be a dwelling.

The limited competition for the Nursing and Biomedical Sciences Building for the University of Texas confronted the Patkau practice with a totally new programmatic and institutional scale. Had this premiated proposal been realized, it would have been not only the architects' largest work to date but also one of their most complex, from the standpoint of the articulation of public and semipublic space. Their earthwork/roofwork theme is relinquished here in favor of a self-contained, largely orthogonal slab, rendered as though it were some kind of landlocked ship. Le Corbusier is an undeniable reference in this regard, notably for his canonical Unité d'Habitation, Marseilles, of 1952.

Part student center, part faculty building, this institution was to have been dedicated to the maintenance of public health, and this may account for its development as a "green" building. The first three floors were recessed from the louvered face of the structure in order to provide a stepped entry portico leading to the student cafeteria, bookstore, and main auditorium. This sequence, fed by a *scala regia,* was to have been separated from an adjacent park by a water-filled moat, which was to have been crossed by ramped passerelles to facilitate access from the campus. This moat, conceived as an integral part of an elaborate recycling system, was connected to a two-story cylindrical rainwater storage tank at the top of the building, fed by the runoff from a photovoltaic shade roof.

This broadening of the office vocabulary did not, however, lead the Patkaus to abandon totally the roofwork thematic with which they made their name. Nowhere is this more evident than in the design of the Gleneagles Community Centre in West Vancouver (2000–2003). Here, the act of building on the gently sloping site entailed an ingenious cut-and-fill operation in order to create a transverse earthwork displacing the section by a single story between the street access on the eastern side of the structure and the lower frontage facing west over a golf course. In this instance, the roofwork floats over the section like a pagoda. Beneath this airy canopy with its deep overhangs are three separate levels, two on the eastern face housing community services—a café, a child-care center, and a meeting room—in conjunction with the administration. These are conveniently accommodated on a reinforced-concrete mezzanine overlooking the three-story height of the gymnasium under a large roof. A fitness center and changing facilities are respectively stacked above and below this mezzanine level.

Like the other pagoda roof-forms in the Patkau practice, this building has been carefully modulated throughout, not only from an environmental standpoint but also with regard to optimizing the economy of its realization. To this end, a concrete manifold and a timber superstructure have been brought together to constitute an efficient assembly from the point of view of maintaining the unity of the institution in relation to the climate. As the architects have aptly put it:

The structural system consists of cast-in-place concrete floor slabs, insulated double-wythe tilt-up concrete end walls, and a heavy timber roof. This structure is an important component of the interior climate-control system of the building: it acts as a huge thermal-storage mass, a giant static heat pump that absorbs, stores, and releases energy to create an extremely stable indoor climate, regardless of the exterior environment. Radiant heating and cooling in both floors and walls maintains a set temperature; the concrete surfaces act alternately as emitters or absorbers. The thermal energy for this system is provided by water-to-water heat pumps via a ground-source heat exchanger under the adjacent parking area. Since air is not used for climate control, opening windows and doors does not affect the performance of the heating and cooling system.[12]

The normative grace and economy of this pagoda surely derives in part from the continuously sweeping line of the curved laminated timber beams and the elegant way in which these are anchored via steel to the central concrete armature and the concrete piers. At the same time, its fugal character as the span and its load pass from wood to steel to concrete is augmented by a thin tubular steel latticework, running in the longitudinal direction, that provides anti-

seismic stiffness to the roof as a whole. The resulting tectonic clarity is heightened by the inner and outer finishing of the roof; inside, prefabricated wooden panels with integrated purlins span between the laminated roof beams, and outside, a standing-seam steel roof covers the well-insulated structure. It is notable that Gleneagles was conceived as a "social condenser" within a highly privatized suburban society.

The biomedical building projected for Texas served as a model for the Grande Bibliothèque in Montreal (2000–2005), the National Library, which was the result of another limited competition in which Patkau Architects received the first prize. Exceptionally compact, this complex structure is clad in a rain screen of horizontal green-glass planks, comparable in their striated figuration to the aluminum louvered skin envisaged for Houston. Like the earlier work, the Quebec library features a major horizontal promenade, along the eastern face of the building. The triple-height, north-south promenade serves to connect the principal threshold functions: the main reception, the central elevator/stair core, the three-hundred-seat lecture hall, the exhibition hall, the meeting rooms, and the primary means of ingress and egress around the elongated perimeter of the building.

Paralleling the rue Berri, this internal street links the boulevard de Maisonneuve subway station to the south of the library to the monumental three-story collection Québécoise in the northeast corner. The library is situated at a particularly prominent intersection in the city fabric, where the east-west boulevard de Maisonneuve crosses the north-south rue Berri. The main entrance, which overlooks the sunken terrace of the children's library, is integrated into the building at exactly this juncture, along with a subterranean link to the subway system. The map room is located at this same point at the top of the building, looking diagonally over the Place du Quartier. Equally topographic in terms of the integration of the library into the preexisting fabric is the western frontage along the avenue Savoie, which has been conceived as a lane to be occupied by second-hand booksellers.

The library is divided into two separate collections, the collection Québécoise and the general collection, both of which are housed in multilevel "wooden boxes" within the glazed enclosure. While the general collection is in the larger of these boxes and is surrounded by

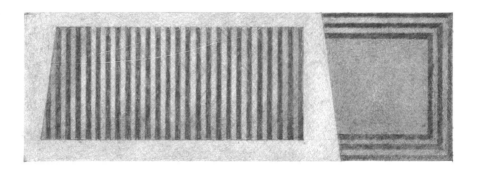

informal reading rooms, the situation in the collection Québécoise is reversed, with a single reading room at the center. One should also note in this regard the two unique, stepped reading rooms that traverse the depth of the block, thereby affording a labyrinthine route through the section that complements the principal means of vertical access by elevator.

The very compactness of the library is contingent on its development as a "building within a building," beginning with the double layering of the glass membrane—rain screen plus curtain wall. This layering is echoed within by the louvered timber walls of the boxes, which encase both the spatial subdivisions and the interstitial gallery levels. The monumental case of the collection Québécoise is permeable so as to permit visual penetration into the seemingly infinite depth of the stacks that surround the main reading volume. Here green-glass table lamps evoke, however incidentally, the eviscerated rotunda that was once the core of the British Museum. However, the ultimate aura of the timber casing is Oriental rather than Occidental, and it is perhaps this bicoastal, referential character that makes this work one of the most cultivated public buildings to have been built in North America in recent years.

The parti of the Grande Bibliothèque is reworked, as it were, in a major addition to the Winnipeg Centennial Library (2002–2005), whereupon it acquires new attributes in terms of the taxonomic organization of the space and the civic identity of the institution. In this regard, the generic stepped reading room of the Montreal library becomes the public spine of the Winnipeg library. At the same time, it is rendered as a curtain-walled conservatory that simultaneously enriches both the library and an adjacent public park. This park/library interface is consummated at grade by a fenced-off section of the park that readers may use in good weather. In Winnipeg, the stepped reading room completes the L-shaped plan of the original library by spanning at forty-five degrees between the two arms.

With the exception of the existing interface with the park, this rather introspective building aligns with both the orthogonal street grid at grade and the enclosed citywide skywalk system, elevated fifteen feet above grade. The fusion of skywalk and library, like the interface between the building and the park, provides direct access from the skywalk to various facilities of the library. An auxiliary

Winnipeg Centennial Library Addition model

Grande Bibliothèque du Québec concept sketch, opposite

reading room overlooks the stepped reading volume descending to the first floor. Finally, one may note that the transparent elevator shafts, the tubular steel columns, and the self-supporting space-frame of the curtain wall facing the park are the three tectonic elements that help one to read the stepped form of the library as a unified public space.

This stepped form again emerges as the *idée fixe* in the Centre for Music, Art, and Design at the University of Manitoba (2002–ongoing), which is rendered as a bridge building, unifying the faculties of architecture, art, and music in a single complex with a common library at the top of the building. In effect, CMAD is rendered as six "big rooms"—library, studio, workshop, production, practice, and exhibition spaces—together with a mediatory volume of unspecified use. These amenities, linked by ramps and stairs, culminate in the stepped reading room of the library, which rises to the top of the four-story structure. As in Winnipeg, the library runs the full length of the main facade. Since this faces south, it is equipped with louvers, by now a typical Patkau trope, providing a striated membrane unifying the overall form.

The newfound typological rationalism of the office acquires a decidedly urban dimension in their proposal for a student residential complex for the campus of the University of Pennsylvania (2004). The most immediately striking aspect of this project is the way in which it completes the block pattern of the campus in relation to the scale of the urban fabric as a whole, thereby redefining the existing green space of Hill Square so as to establish a definite boundary between the Penn campus and the western edge of Drexel University. By enclosing the northern and eastern edges of the green space (Chestnut Street and Thirty-third Street) with eight-story residential slabs, the architects terminated a diagonal northeast-southwest campus path while still relating to the mass-form of the existing Hill College House student residence designed by Eero Saarinen. The site plan comprises two residential blocks set at right angles to one another straddling the northeastern entry into the campus. These blocks are linked by a passerelle at the first floor.

The typology of the proposed new dormitory is effectively a subtle upgrading of the traditional Oxbridge "gyp room" pattern, wherein a number of private rooms are gathered about common cooking and toilet facilities. In order to eliminate the long, double-loaded corridors so typical of student housing, the Patkau practice envisaged a permutation of suites of rooms, ranging from four to six rooms in length, arranged along a central corridor so that three successive suites open to a double-height common living space on every other floor. Each of the common rooms is accompanied by a generous terrace of equal depth and area, and the plan pattern is such that adjacent terraces, on different sides of the block, are interconnected by passerelles, thereby permitting pedestrian movement between twelve suites over every two floors. This number corresponds to the number of suites under the supervision of a single house master. The passerelles cross through vertical airshafts at each overlap in plan, thereby both ventilating the accommodation and providing for social interaction over a larger range. Of this scalar hierarchy the architects have written:

The spatial structure of the residential facilities reflects the social structure, resulting in a hierarchy of spaces. Major urban spaces such as Hill Square collect the university and surrounding population; ground-level social and service spaces gather the College House community as a whole; lounges within clusters focus an intermediate scale of group; suites identify the basic social unit, which includes the individual student room. This hierarchy both constructs a finely grained and scaled community and supports privacy, promoting group definition as well as personal needs.[13]

This subtle sociospatial formation prompted the architects to devise an equally permutable pattern of fenestration for the student rooms. The building is faced in full-height, prefabricated, modular panels, and the resultant fenestration pattern is further syncopated by tinted-glass rain shields that add an overlay to the basic play between solid and void. By way of contrast, the ground and first floors, devoted to collective social facilities, are faced with large sheets of plate glass.

From a civic point of view, both the Penn campus proposal and the project for University Square on the University of British Columbia campus in Vancouver (2005) envisage continuous medium-rise developments containing and hence modulating rather large spaces. While the two plans are conceived as reinforcing the urban grain, the University Square project is subtly rendered as an urban landscape

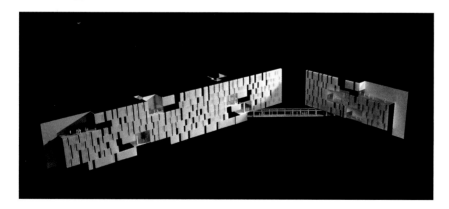

New College House
building envelope concept

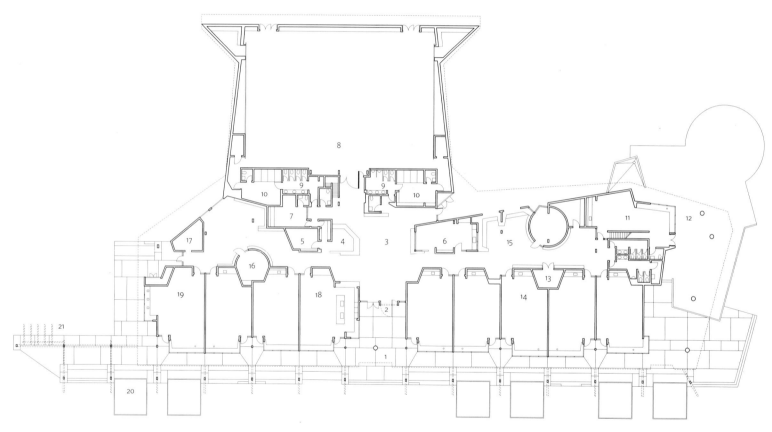

1 entrance porch
2 entrance
3 common area
4 reception
5 principal
6 staff room
7 health/counselling
8 gym/community hall
9 washrooms
10 showers/change
11 kindergarten

12 covered play area
13 storage
14 classroom
15 library/resource area
16 reading room
17 workroom
18 home economics room
19 science room
20 teaching gardens
21 drying racks

0   20 ft

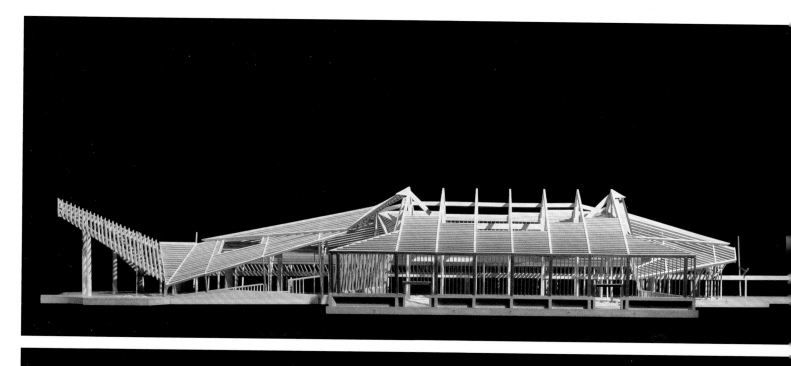

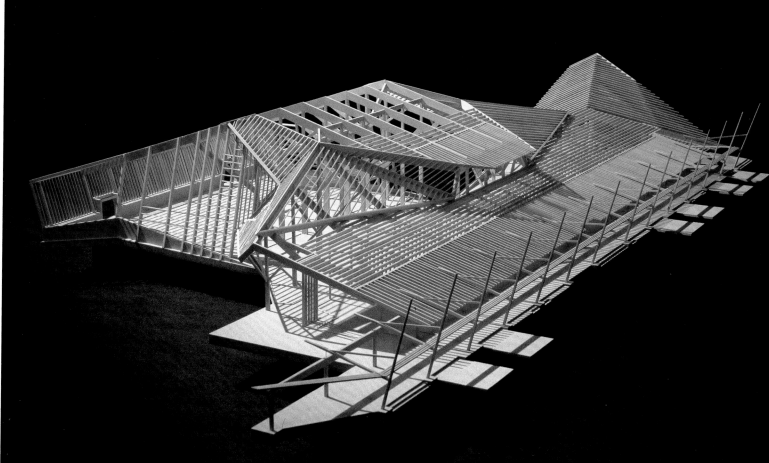

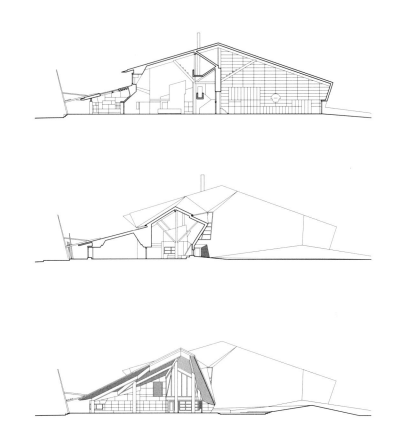

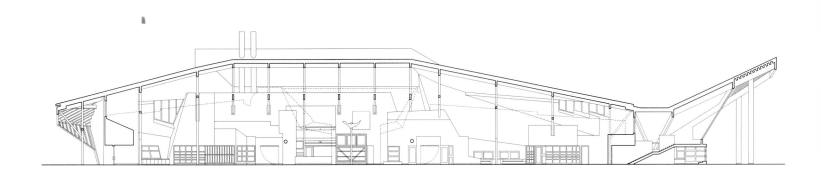

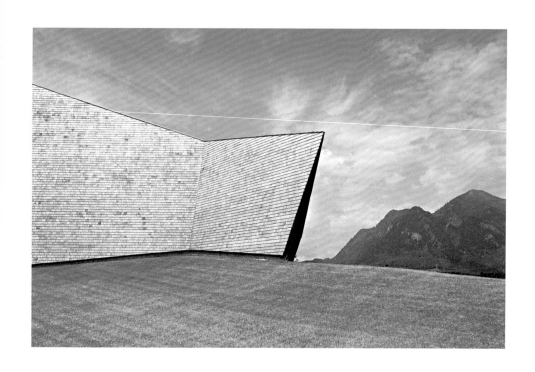

Canadian Clay and Glass Gallery
Waterloo, Ontario, 1988–1992

The modern archetype of the museum interior is the white cube: a pure space, artificially lit, with no connection to the exterior. This model has risen in response both to curatorial interests and to the increasing abstraction of avant-garde painting and sculpture in the postwar period. Characteristically this type of space tends to isolate art from everyday life.

The design of the Canadian Clay and Glass Gallery, which was the winning entry in an invited design competition in 1986, challenges both the universality and the isolation of this stereotype. Idiosyncratic elements and spaces such as the tower gallery, the small works gallery, and the courtyard gallery have been inserted within the main gallery to place spectator and art object in a specific, intensified architectural relationship. To take advantage of the robust nature of clay and glass under light, museum interiors are strongly connected to the exterior. Natural light from skylights, windows, and the courtyard articulates gallery

spaces and brings daily and seasonal cycles inside. Views of the exterior animate displays of stained glass with changing light and movement.

The construction of the museum is straightforwardly expressed to create a context within which the materiality and craft of clay and glass artworks can be considered. A simple hierarchy of building materials evidences the place of various architectural elements within the order of the building. Primary elements are constructed of more durable and difficult to construct materials. Details reveal the layers of construction, articulating the relationships between materials. The floor plinth, tower gallery, small works gallery, and courtyard gallery are exposed concrete. Concrete masonry bearing walls, exposed to the interior, support roof and floor assemblies of wood decking on steel beams. Exterior walls are clad with brick veneer, detailed at openings to express the composite nature of contemporary building assemblies. Door and window frames are wood.

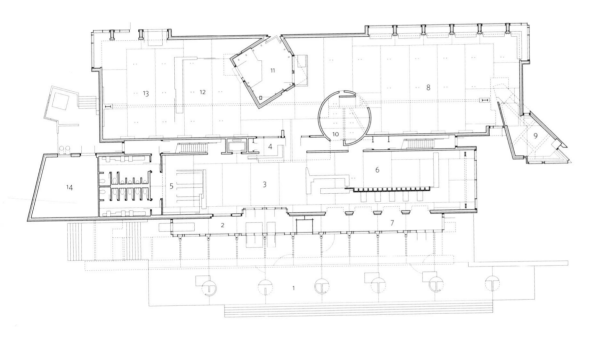

Upper level

1 secretary/reception
2 director
3 curator
4 educator
5 docents
6 janitor
7 library/archives
8 reading room/board room
9 librarian
10 workroom
11 kitchenette
12 open to below
13 mechanical room

Main level

1 gas-fired light columns
2 entry vestibule
3 lobby
4 information/ticket desk
5 cloakroom
6 gift shop
7 tea room
8 main gallery
9 tower gallery
10 small works gallery
11 courtyard gallery
12 demonstration/adjudication
13 support facilities
14 mechanical/electrical room

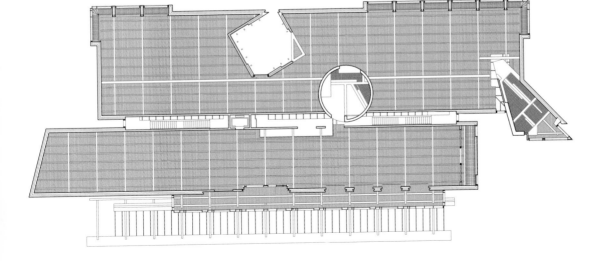

0   20 ft

38

After the design of the gallery was completed, a model study was undertaken to continue the exploration of the formal principles of the design. The model represents an irregular segment taken from the center of the building. The open-ended and fragmentary nature of the model allows characteristics of the design, such as the play of complex linear constructions against simple geometric volumes and the layering of components within building assemblies, to be made more explicit. In addition, the partial nature of the model suggests unexpected formal possibilities—largely independent of the original design—for the densely centered but open-ended composition and for the juxtaposition of complete and fragmentary forms.

Newton Library
Surrey, British Columbia, 1990–1992

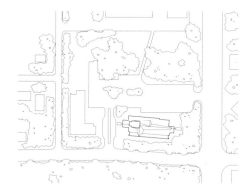

The site for this single-story neighborhood library is located in a context of suburban strip malls and residential subdivisions. It is difficult in this visually competitive and chaotic environment for a small library to achieve an appropriate public presence, so the perimeter walls to the north and south are exaggerated in height. Not only does this give the building greater authority on the street, it also allows large amounts of controlled natural light to enter the building. The south side is layered and shaped to control the sometimes harsh southern sun; the glass curtain wall on the north allows soft light to fill the interior with a quiet luminosity.

Unlike the north and south perimeter walls, the entrance, which is to the west, adjacent to the principal vehicular access to the site, is compressed, even intimate. This compression creates inward-sloping roof planes that meet in a "valley." The valley runs the length of the building, maintaining the scale of the entrance along the

primary circulation spine; the inward-sloping ceiling planes help drive natural daylight from the high sidewalls deep into the interior.

The central compression, in conjunction with a pitched attic space above the roof, also provides a plenum for air distribution ducts. These ducts lead from a mechanical penthouse located directly above the entrance along the valley. The attic diminishes in size as distance from the penthouse increases and number and size of ducts decrease. The interrelationship between attic and valley results in a cross-slope that drains the entire roof to each end of the building. Water is directed through large galvanized-steel scuppers into rock-filled catchment areas on grade and is then allowed to percolate back into the water table of the site.

The structural system consists of a laminated timber frame on a concrete foundation. The open expressive quality of this tectonic system establishes the primary character of the building

shell and extends outside as a rain canopy. However, concrete and timber absorb rather than reflect light, especially in this region where the light can be very soft under the frequently overcast skies of winter. Thus a complementary system of light-reflecting cladding is added to both interior and exterior where a more luminous or enclosing character is required. Inside, white-painted gypsum board ceilings reflect light into the large open collection and reading areas. On the exterior, bright yellow stucco-clad walls cover the portions of the tectonic frame that enclose perimeter offices, meeting rooms, and service rooms.

This model study is an exploration of the formal principles of the building design and the sectional extensions of these principles. Such investigations, notably in relation to the ground plane, were not possible in the actual building due to considerations of security and accessibility.

The model consists of two components that represent the dialectical nature of the design: the tectonic portion of the building and the clad portion of the building. Taken individually, each element corresponds with a complete architectural schema. Taken together, they suggest a more complex, transformational schema that is capable of responding to a diverse physical and conceptual context.

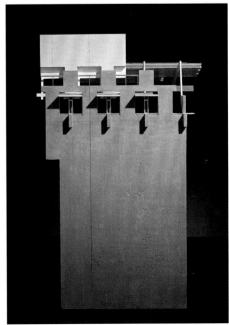

Barnes House

Nanaimo, British Columbia, 1991–1993

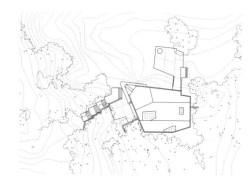

The Barnes house is located on Vancouver Island within a forested five-acre parcel of land; the building is lodged into a crevice at the edge of an open rocky outcrop that overlooks the Strait of Georgia and the British Columbia mainland beyond. The experience of the site begins within the intimacy and shade of the forest and expands beyond the outcrop and the surrounding vegetation to encompass the region centered on the strait. Different places within the house focus on different aspects of this experience, from the small-scale textural characteristics of rock and vegetation to the large-scale expanse of the sea.

The irregular and variable spaces, sequence, and massing of the house derive directly from the variable natural characteristics of the site. The geometry of plan and section is subtly inflected to fit the building into its crevice and to connect to rock, trees, and clearings within the forest. Walls and mass transform from closed and inde-terminate in the forest to open and geometric in the clearing. Window openings on the lower level carefully direct the view into rock or to the base of trees and the forest floor, while windows on the upper level look into groves of arbutus or fir and cedar or out over the strait to a panorama of water and mainland mountains.

Building materials, each used in the manner and purpose for which it is most suitable, are similarly variable. Within an envelope of stud-frame walls, clad on the exterior with stucco and on the interior with painted gypsum board, three con-crete columns rise to support a heavy timber roof structure. Steel—in elaborated connections between concrete and heavy timber, in stair rail-ings, and in the entrance canopy—provides a counterpoint to the concrete, timber, and mono-lithic clad-wood framing. The entrance canopy, formed from a three-eighths-inch-thick steel plate, cantilevers twelve feet over the entry door and a large window facing northwest.

Strawberry Vale School
Victoria, British Columbia, 1992–1995

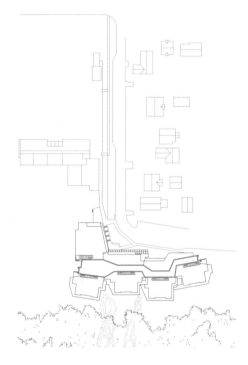

Strawberry Vale School is a public school for students from kindergarten to grade seven. The site is in a semirural area on the outskirts of Victoria and immediately north of a Garry oak woodland, a rare and delicate ecosystem unique to the region. The design of the school is inspired by the environmental knowledge embedded in the vernacular language of rural buildings; like such buildings, the structure aspires to give architectural form to natural forces.

Sixteen classrooms are grouped in pods of four and oriented toward the south to optimize natural lighting and to facilitate an intimate connection with the woodland. To minimize site disturbance, the location and elevation of each pod is adjusted to follow the contours of the land and avoid rock outcroppings. A meandering circulation spine results from this ad hoc placement of classroom pods. The irregular configuration of spine and pods creates a variety of nonprogrammed spaces that support educational and social interactions

both spontaneous and planned, thereby providing an architectural basis for a stronger sense of community within the school.

The hydrology and biodiversity of the site are carefully developed to mediate the environmental impact of the school. The hydrological cycle begins on the south side of the building, where rainwater is collected in concrete trenches below roof overhangs. This water is piped to the lower, north side of the school, where it is discharged into a landscape swale. The swale is planted with rough grass that will gradually be taken over by aquatic plants brought by birds, wind, and the occasional class of students. At the low point of the site, water collects in a shallow marsh. Classes use this area to plant and monitor cattails, bulrushes, and plant species collected from neighboring marshlands. Here also, the microbial growth attached to water plants filters and cleans water from the site and the building before it seeps back into the subsurface water of the area.

The natural systems acting on the building contribute to the heating, ventilation, and lighting systems of the school: heating by simple passive heat gain when sun angles are low; lighting via the controlled placement of windows, clerestories, and skylights along with reflective interior surfaces that distribute sunlight evenly; and ventilation through the stack effect inherent in the building cross section. Materials minimize the amount of energy that is embodied within the building. Wood, the most readily accessible and renewable construction resource in the region, is the principal material. Walls and roofs are both framed and sheathed with wood. Recycled steel is used where structural requirements exceed the capacity of second-growth lumber sizes. Foundations and floors are reinforced concrete. Interior claddings and finishes are kept to a minimum, leaving exposed much of the primary construction of wood, steel, and concrete.

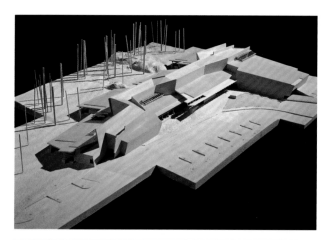

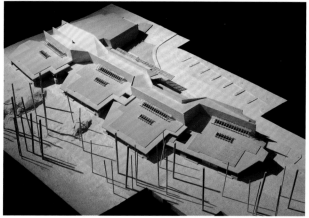

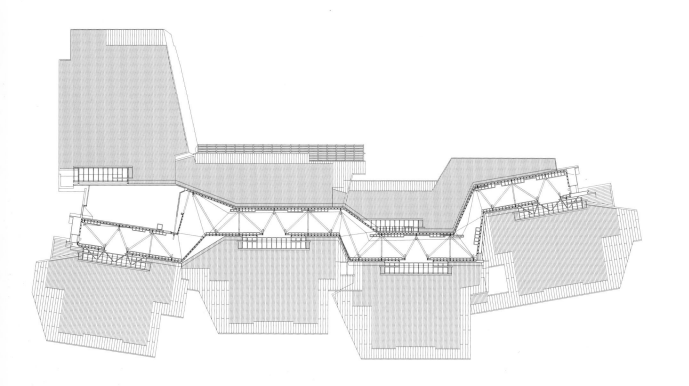

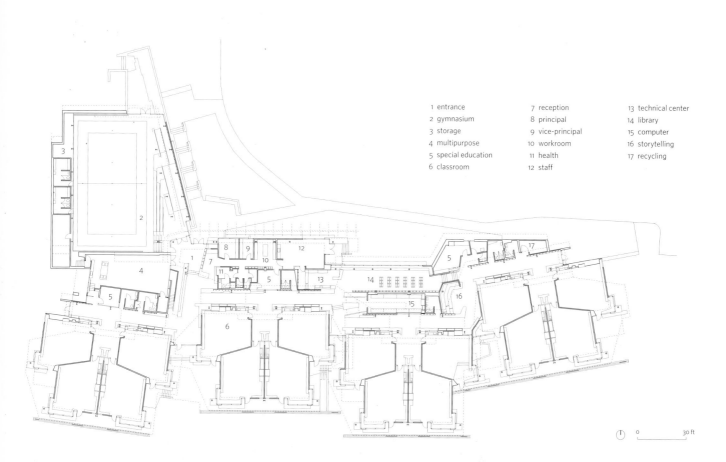

1 entrance
2 gymnasium
3 storage
4 multipurpose
5 special education
6 classroom

7 reception
8 principal
9 vice-principal
10 workroom
11 health
12 staff

13 technical center
14 library
15 computer
16 storytelling
17 recycling

0   30 ft

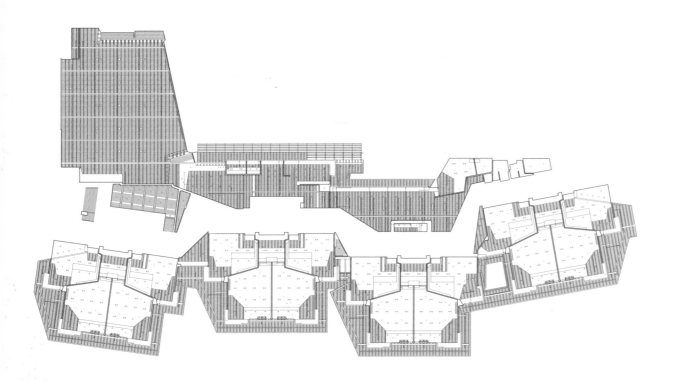

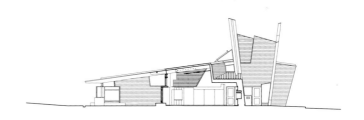

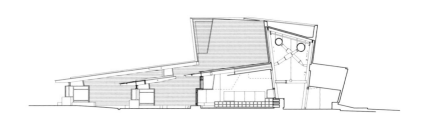

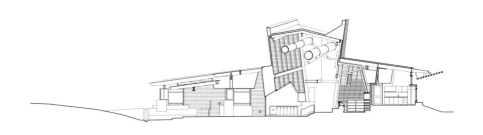

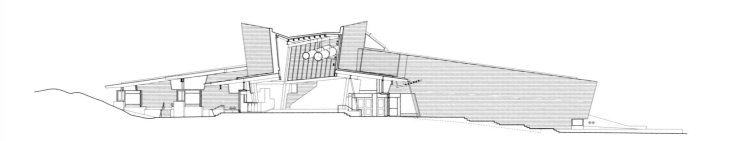

Strawberry Vale School
Analytical Model

This model investigates a number of themes that evolved in the projects leading to the Strawberry Vale School: the role of the particular in the context of an increasingly generalized international culture; material, organizational, and spatial differentiation within building systems; and pragmatism as an approach to architectural form. The fragmentary and open-ended nature of the model facilitates the study of these interests, while the formal qualities that result suggest that the areas of exploration implicit in its design, and the building from which it is extrapolated, lead inevitably toward a study of heterogeneity.

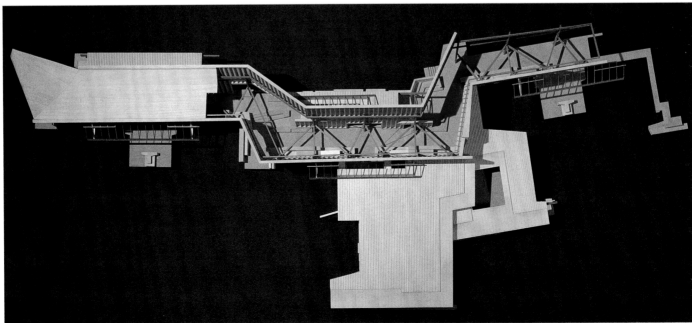

Shaw House

Vancouver, British Columbia, 1995–2000

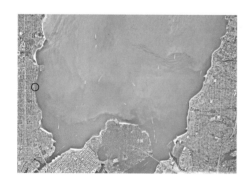

The Shaw house is located on a narrow waterfront property on the south shore of English Bay. Views from the site stretch across the bay to encompass the skyline of downtown Vancouver and, beyond, the mountains on the north shore of the bay. The house is organized with living spaces at grade, a music room below, and a single bedroom, study, and lap pool above. The pool, with terraces at each end, runs along the entire west side of the house.

Because the house is so narrow, spatial expansion is possible only outward over the water and upward. Generous ceiling heights enlarge spaces; a clerestory above the lap pool transmits daylight and dappled, reflected light deep into the central spaces, including the dining room, which rises from the ground level to the upper level of the house. The entrance is directly under the pool, midway along the side of the house. An almost magical aqueous light is transmitted to the entrance area through the water and glass bottom of the pool.

Like many cities on the West Coast, Vancouver is in an area of high seismic risk. A robust structure is required to resist the significant lateral forces that would result from the large mass of water in the pool in the event of an earthquake. Thus the house is constructed almost entirely of reinforced concrete. A special dense mix utilizing white cement keeps the structure looking bright during frequent rainy weather. Inside this concrete shell, the house is insulated and clad with gypsum board. In areas where insulation is not required, the concrete structure is exposed. Muted materials and colors—white-painted walls, pale concrete floors, precast stair treads, and bleached millwork—allow natural light, even the soft light of winter, to describe the interior.

1 entry
2 dining room
3 living room
4 kitchen
5 powder room
6 garage
7 bedroom

8 bathroom
9 guest bathroom
10 study
11 lap pool
12 hot pool
13 music room
14 light well

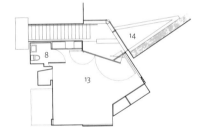

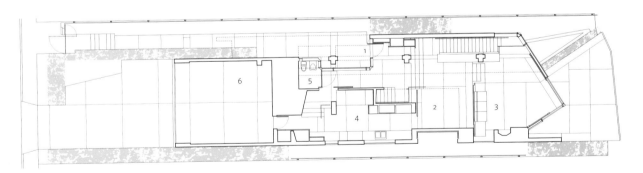

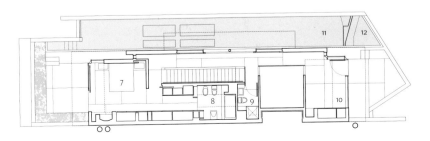

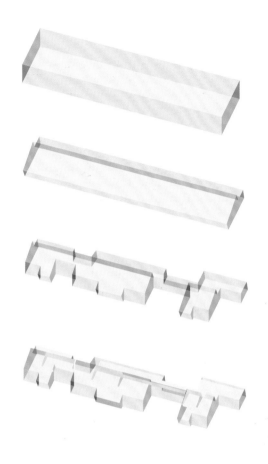

The Agosta house sits in a grassy meadow enclosed on three sides by forty-three acres of second-growth Douglas fir forest. The fourth side of the meadow opens to the northwest, where it overlooks rolling fields and, across Haro Strait in the distance, the Gulf Islands of British Columbia. The house includes a separate structure with an office and guest quarters and also a vegetable and flower garden, which is protected from the numerous deer on San Juan Island by a twelve-foot fence.

The structure, which spans the ridge of the meadow, forms a "dam" that divides the site. An enclosed forecourt to the southeast suggests a spatial reservoir to be released through the house; a panoramic view to the northwest becomes a spatial sea of picturesque fields and waterways. In section, walls and roof are sloped to respond to the gentle but steady incline of the site. The organization of the house is the result of extruding and then manipulating this section,

either by erosion, which produces exterior in-between spaces that divide the house programmatically, or by insertion, which uses ceiling bulkheads to separate the programmatic areas created by the exterior in-between spaces into more finely scaled interior areas.

The construction of the house is simple in concept—a wood frame on a concrete slab. It is intended to have the direct quality of a rural or even agricultural building. In execution, the construction is somewhat more sophisticated. The structure is a combination of exposed heavy timber framing and conventional stud framing; the interior is clad in white-painted gypsum board. Radiant heating is embedded in the simple concrete slab foundation. Most exterior surfaces are clad in light-gauge galvanized sheet steel, which protects the structure not only from the weather but from forest wildfires.

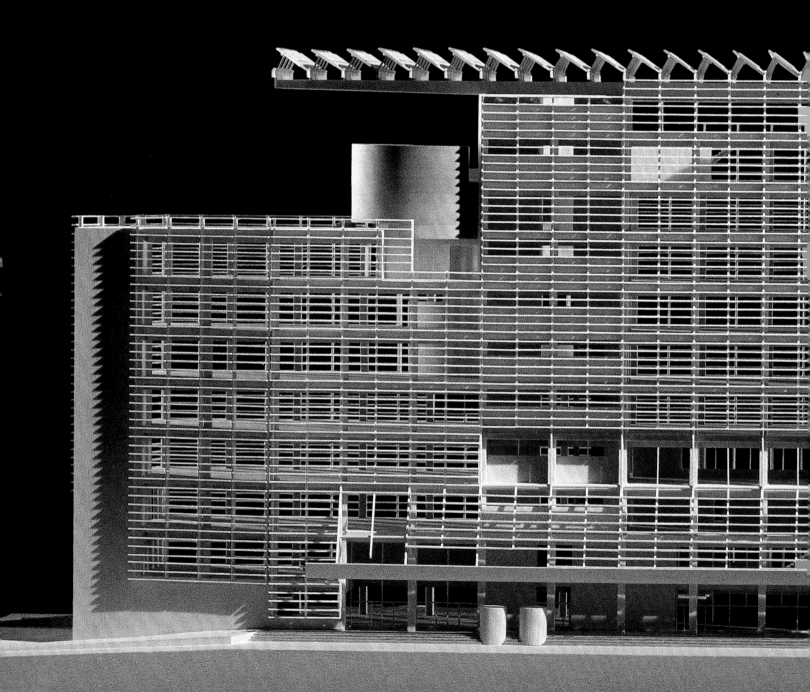

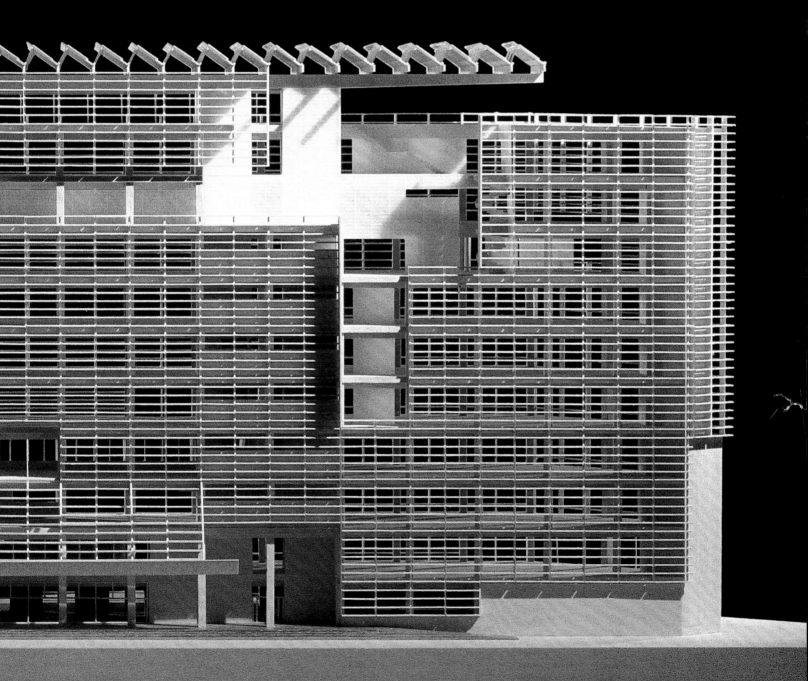

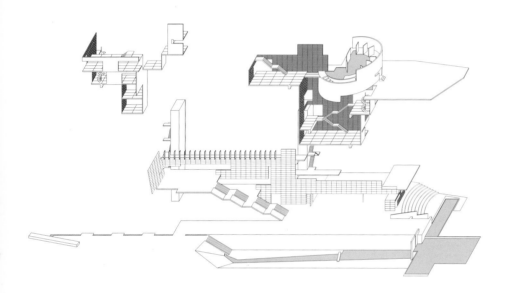

The University of Texas Houston Health Science Center is one of more than forty institutions that make up the Texas Medical Center, the largest, most densely developed medical complex in the United States. The Nursing and Biomedical Sciences Building, the winning project in an invited design competition, is located on a narrow east-west plot adjacent to Grant Fay Park, the last remaining green space within the medical center.

The size of the site and the large, complex program, along with a desire to preserve the park, call for a high-rise building. Yet this typology seems inherently at odds with the academic life of a university. High-rises tend to limit social interaction by isolating building occupants on separate floors and at the same time separating them from the surrounding urban context. To counteract these conditions, various floors within the building are connected by multistory volumes, typically public or social spaces, that allow people to congregate, to see activity on different

levels, and to circulate between levels without relying exclusively on elevators. The bookstore, student services, major auditorium, dining hall, classrooms, and student lounges are located within, or connected by, a four-story loggia at grade; in good weather, the loggia opens to the park. On upper levels interconnected exterior terraces, carved out of the volume of the building, connect faculty meeting rooms and lounges and extend to roof terraces adjacent to a conference center. An irregular system of interior and exterior stairs, rising through the height of the building, connects these spaces to reinforce their role in gathering the academic community.

The climate of Houston is semitropical. Much of the year is characterized by intense sun, heat, and high humidity; torrential rains storm in from the Gulf of Mexico every summer. The impact of this climate on the building, and the impact of the building on the environment, is mediated in part by a layered building envelope. A system

of operable horizontal louvers shades east- and west-facing glass walls. The fields of louvers both characterize the building elevations and establish a context for exception. Against this field, the idiosyncratic social and public spaces, which can be seen on the facades, speak— literally—of the academic identity of the building. For most of the day, the louvers are in an open, horizontal position. In this orientation, they not only shade building faces but also reflect daylight into building interiors. Coupled with the narrow building width, this use of ambient light allows most interior spaces to be naturally illuminated for substantial periods of time. The louvers may be closed, on either side, for short periods to prevent solar heat gain in the early morning or late evening when the sun is low in the sky or for extended periods to shield the glass walls during storms. Because the louvers are made of perforated metal, building occupants can see to the exterior when the louver system is closed.

La Petite Maison du Weekend
1998–1999

Constructed for the "Fabrications" exhibition at the Wexner Center for the Arts, in Columbus, Ohio, La Petite Maison du Weekend is a prototype for a self-sufficient dwelling. Intended as minimal accommodation for a weekend getaway for two, it can be located on virtually any outdoor site, including remote, unserviced locations, and will provide the basics for everyday life: shelter, sleeping loft, kitchen, shower, and toilet.

La Petite Maison du Weekend generates its own electricity, collects and distributes rainwater, and composts waste using only the natural dynamics of the site. Materials and premanufactured components include a composite plywood-and-timber shell, steel base and superstructure, glass and photovoltaic roof, canvas water reservoir, composting toilet, gravity shower and kitchen sink, small battery bank, high-performance refrigerator, low-voltage lighting, and small propane burner. Major components are intended to be manufactured in the shop and assembled on the site.

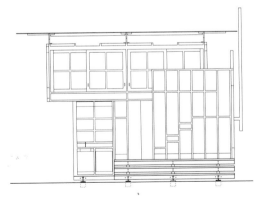 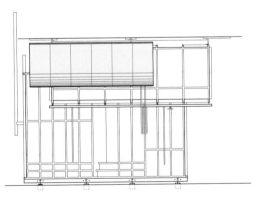

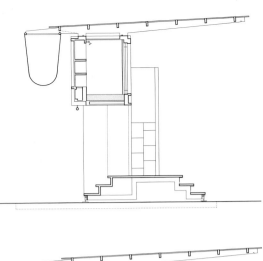

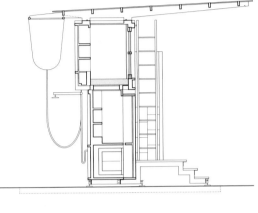

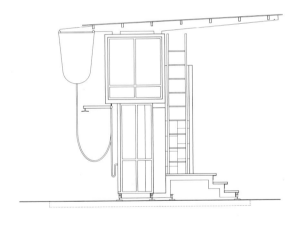

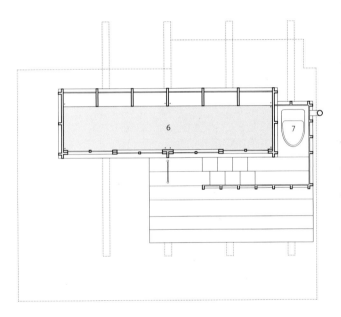

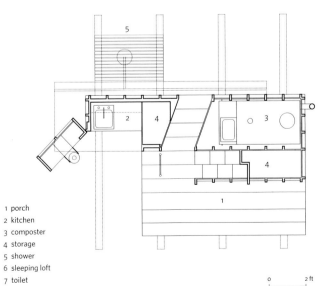

1 porch
2 kitchen
3 composter
4 storage
5 shower
6 sleeping loft
7 toilet

0   2 ft

Grande Bibliothèque du Québec
Montreal, Quebec, 2000–2005

The Grande Bibliothèque du Québec, the winning entry in an international design competition, consolidates a number of collections dispersed throughout the province to create a resource library for the region as well as a central public library for the city of Montreal. Four hundred thousand square feet in size, the building contains four major components: a general library, a children's library, the collection Québécoise (historic documents pertaining to Quebec), and an assortment of public spaces outside the library control zone. The building is located in Montreal's Latin Quarter, between boulevard de Maisonneuve and rue Ontario, diagonally opposite the green space of place du Quartier. Below grade, the library is joined to a major intersection in the Montreal metro system.

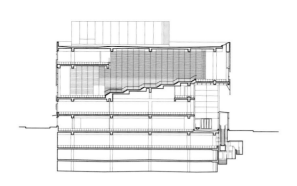

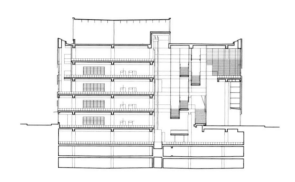

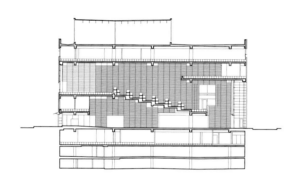

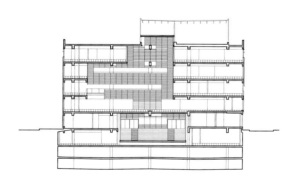

The Centre for Music, Art, and Design is an inter-disciplinary facility at the University of Manitoba shared by the Faculties of Architecture and Music, the School of Fine Art, and the integrated Architecture, Fine Art, and Music Library. The new building joins two existing buildings to form an arts courtyard with buildings on three sides and an important cross-campus pedestrian corridor on the fourth. CMAD is the new public face of the university arts community, decisively broadcasting its activities on campus.

The University of Manitoba is just south of Winnipeg on the Red River; winter temperatures routinely drop well below zero. As in many places with extreme winter weather, a network of underground tunnels complements a network of surface pathways. CMAD interweaves these dual urban conditions. At grade, entrances strategically intersect pedestrian routes. Below grade, the building extends the campus tunnel network by providing links to the previously isolated recreation facilities, parking, and School of Music, as well as allowing for future links. The direct connections to neighboring buildings, both above- and belowground, support informal social inter-action, ease the sharing of resources, and allow for large-scale public events.

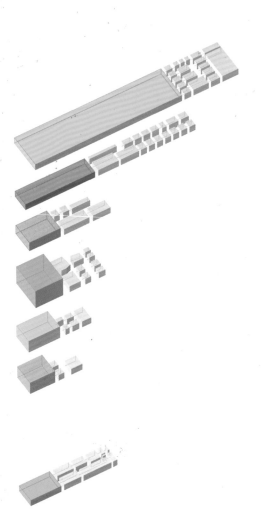

The program was conceived to achieve functional objectives and interdisciplinary ambitions with economy. Instead of a one-to-one association between spaces and uses, CMAD proposes a many-many correspondence. Six "big rooms," named by purpose, accommodate multiple activities: Library, Studio, Workshop, Production, Practice, and Exhibition. Technical support spaces accompany the big rooms. Since they are shared and multiuse, the big rooms foster collaboration between disciplines.

As an antipode to the intensely occupied big rooms, the program allocates space to no program at all, "Mix Space." Mix Space supports the unexpected and serendipitous interaction essential to learning and research. The six big rooms and Mix Space are assembled spatially to multiply possibilities for interconnection and overlap. Distributed nonhierarchically over four levels, the rooms function both individually and collectively. Relationships in plan and section

create a vibrant, urban interior that is richly (and sometimes unexpectedly) illuminated with natural light.

Exhibition, the most public of the big rooms, is on the ground floor, adjacent to public thoroughfares on grade. Library is on the upper two levels so that it benefits from access to daylight. Production, Practice, Workshop, and Studio are all below grade at the tunnel level. A working group, these four big rooms complement each other and neighbor facilities in adjacent buildings. A below-grade courtyard on the west side of the building provides public presence and natural light to the tunnel-level spaces.

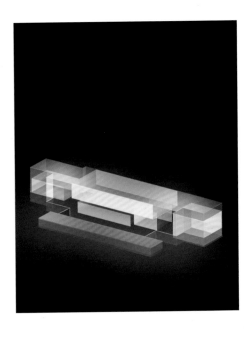

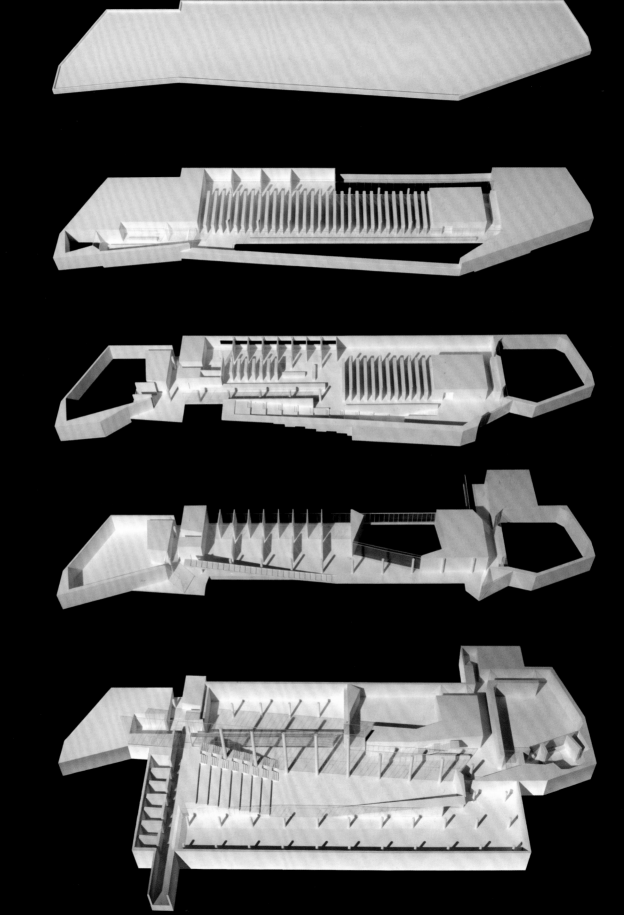

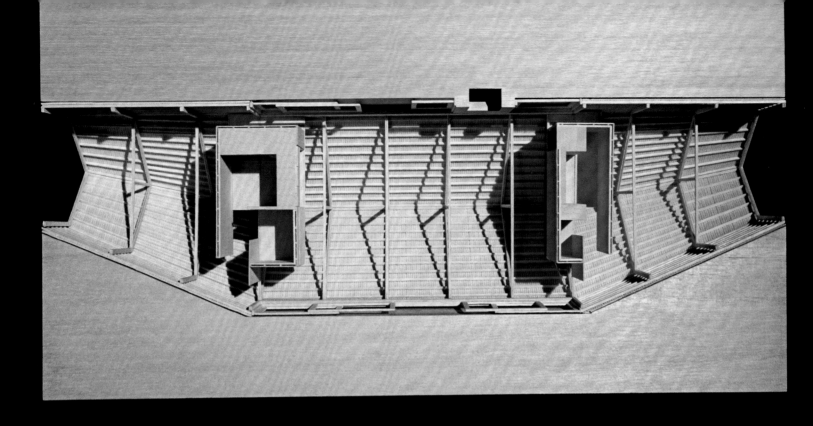

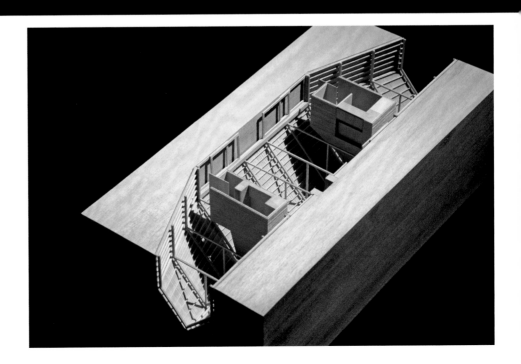

205

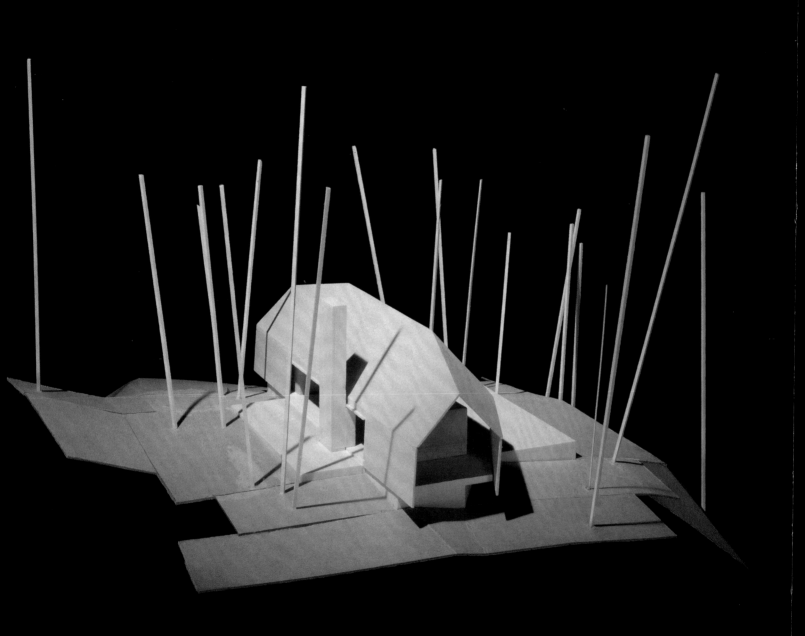

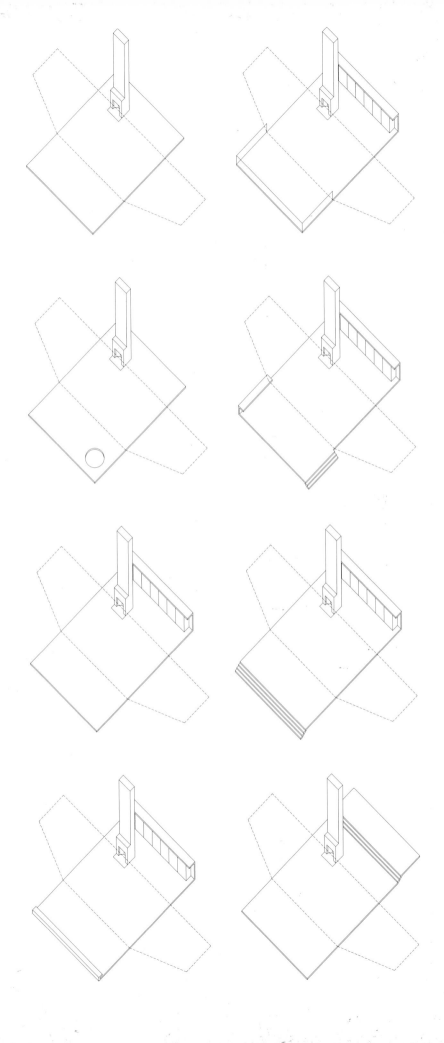

Little House
West Vancouver, British Columbia, 2004–

The Little house is located in a forested mountainside suburb of Vancouver. The site looks south over the Burrard Inlet harbor, downtown Vancouver, Stanley Park, English Bay, and the University of British Columbia campus beyond.

A concrete retaining wall carves a volume out of the slope of the site to describe the boundaries of the house. Within this perimeter, the house is organized on three levels, each with a different spatial condition. The lowest level has modest openings in walls; light is filtered through a pool and glass floor above. This watery, subterranean light marks the entrance spaces of the house; guest room, media room, service rooms, garage, and staff room are also located on this level. A concrete stair rises along the retaining wall at the back of the entry to family spaces on the main level of the house. Space flows horizontally, bounded but barely held by the retaining wall; on this level, the living room, dining room, kitchen, and fitness area are continuous with an exterior court and expand to the south to include panoramic views of the city and ocean below. The stair continues along the retaining wall, rising above the sloping ground, to the upper level of the house. This volume, which contains family bedrooms and a study, floats above the site but is strictly bounded by aluminum grilles that screen extensive glazing to provide privacy and mediate the relationship between interior and exterior.

Pale and luminous materials maximize the soft natural light of the region. Within the boundary of the light gray concrete retaining wall, water and glass, white-painted interior partitions, bleached-wood cabinetry and floors, and aluminum ceilings, soffits, and grilles form a diffuse, moth-toned palette.

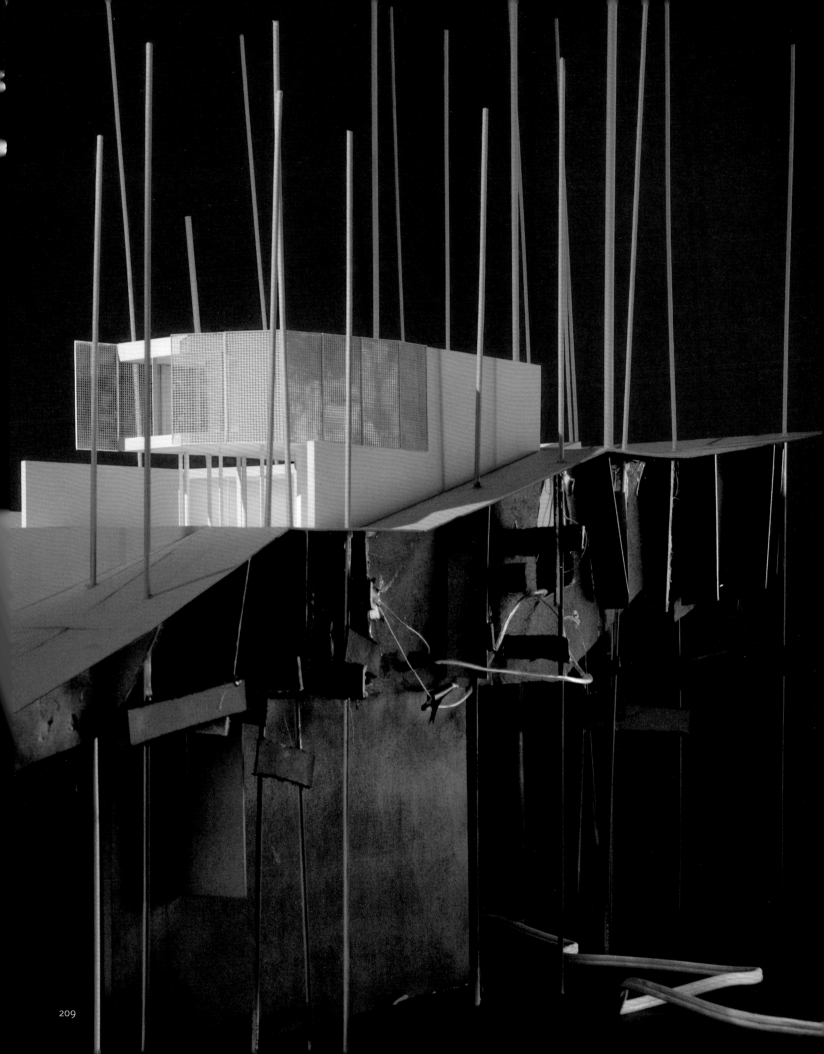

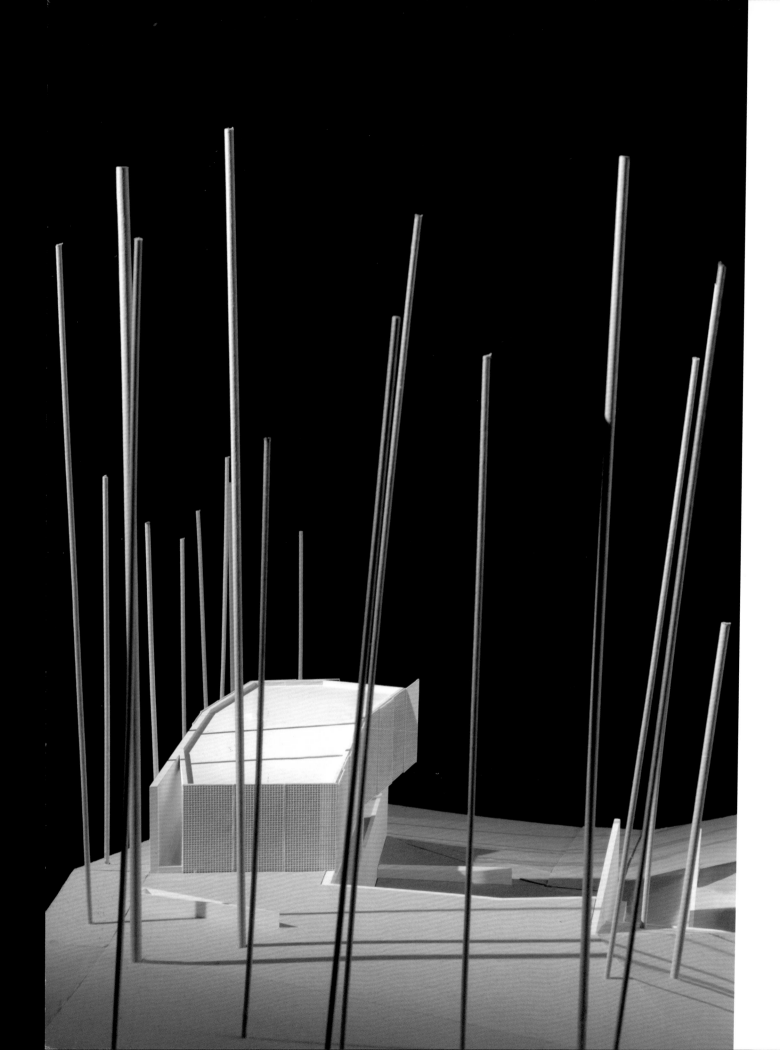

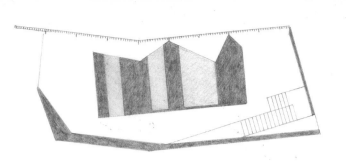

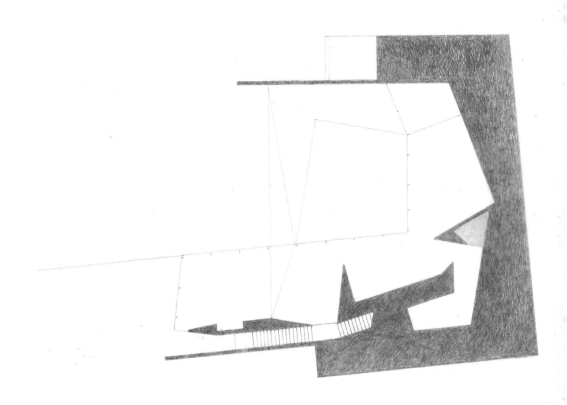

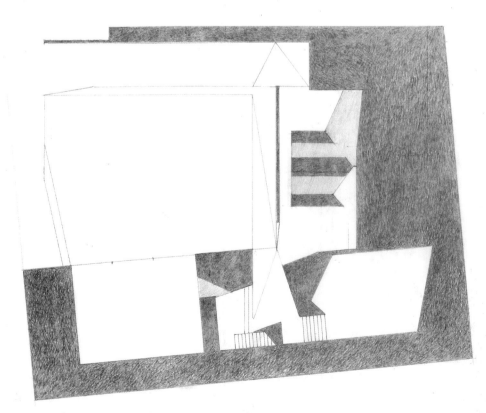

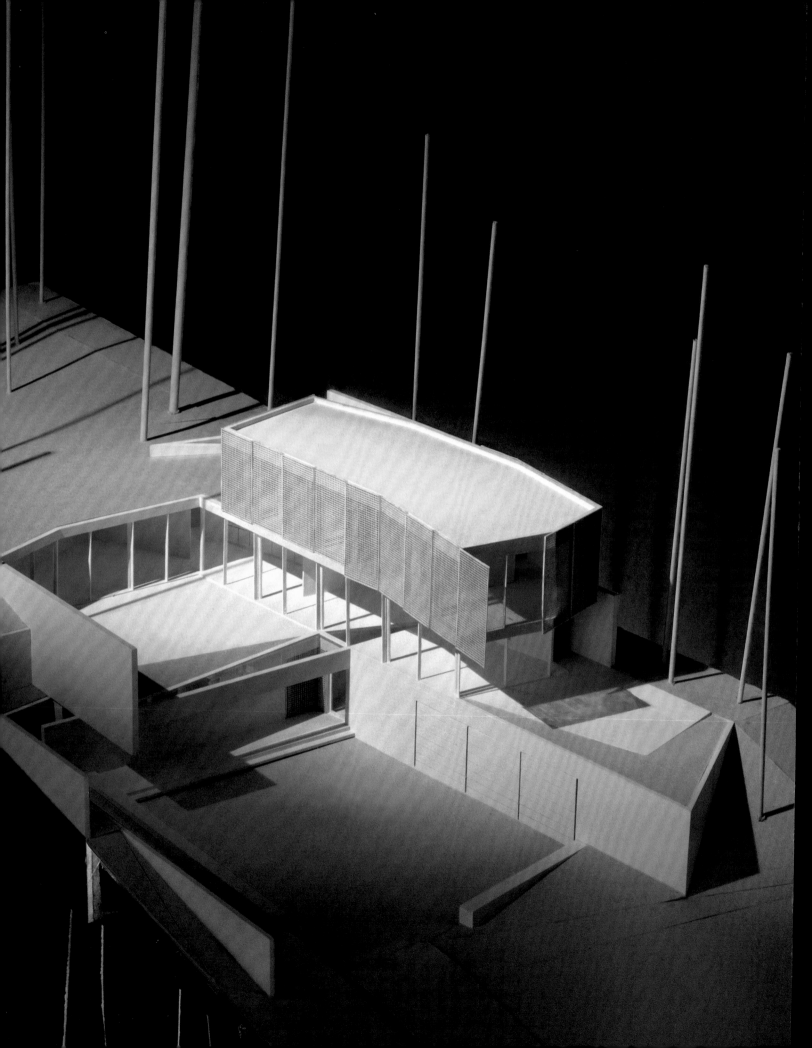

population; ground-level social and service spaces gather the College House community as a whole; lounges within clusters focus an intermediate scale of group; suites identify the basic social unit, which includes the individual student room. This hierarchy both constructs a finely grained and scaled community and supports privacy, promoting group definition as well as personal needs.

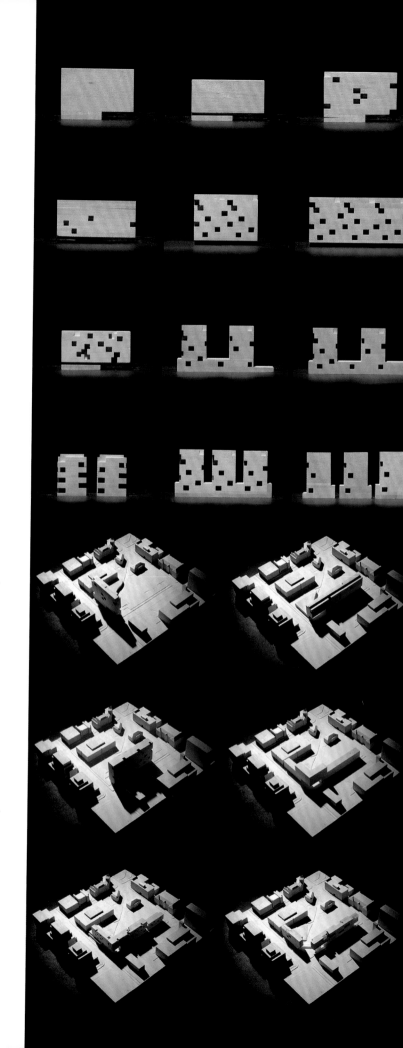

Originally, a small triangular site within Hill Square was designated for the student residence. Accommodating the program in this location would have required an eighteen-story building, exacerbating the formal heterogeneity of the square, creating an awkward relationship to Hill College House, and shading a great deal of the surrounding area.

An alternate site, along two sides of the square, allows the new facility to define open space in the manner of the historic campus and with significantly reduced shading. Narrow eight-story "bar" buildings along Chestnut Street to the north and Thirty-third Street to the east bring the heterogeneous context together. The northeast corner is left open to establish an entrance to the campus and to preserve the public nature of the square. A glass-enclosed bridge, which provides internal connection between the two buildings, spans this opening to further define the spatial character of the campus gateway.

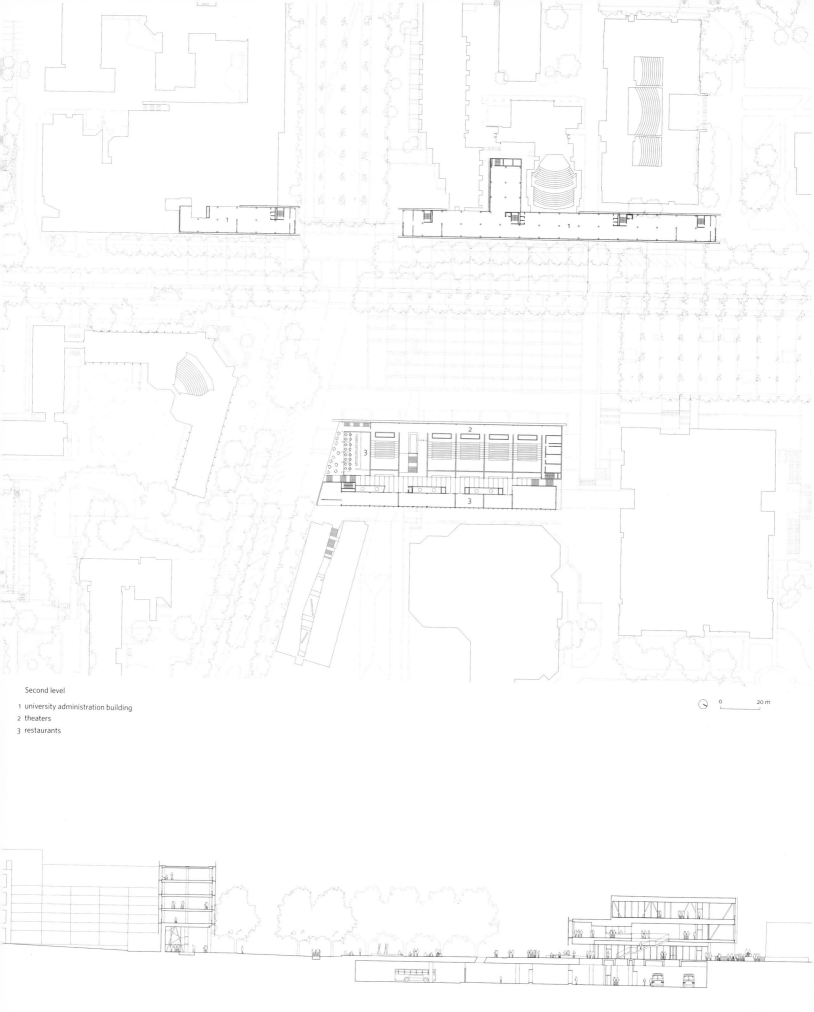

Second level

1 university administration building
2 theaters
3 restaurants

0   20 m

Collaborators

Omer Arbel
Kenneth Arboe
Laura Arpiainen
Paula Barclay
Tina Becker
Andrea Beckum
Vaughn Berg
Tom Bessai
Oliver Birett
Shawn Bleet
Janet Bloomberg
Christoph Boeckeler
Eric Boelling
Greg Boothroyd
Win Bruckshaw
Brad Cameron
Grace Cheung
Judy Cheung
Stephan Chevalier
Shelley Craig
Michael Cunningham
Martin Davidson
Maria Denegri
Gina Dhein
Elaine Didyk
Anike Duffner
Dominique Dumais
Michael Elkan
Robert Fabijaniak
Daryl Favor
Joanne Gates
Jeff Gilliard
Gregory Graemiger
Josie Grant
Tony Griffin
Wan Fa Guo

Bruce Haden
Felix Harbig
Samantha Hayes
Juliane Heinrich
Anders Hellum
Michael Jacobson
Greg Johnson
Laura Killam
David Kosdruy
Michael Kothke
Dimitri Koubatis
Maureen Kwong
Julie LaFreneire
Horace Lai
Andrew Larigakis
Michael Leckie
Thomas Lee
Brendon Levitt
Hector Lo
Mitra Mansour
Imke Maron
Davis Marques
Kayna Merchant
Stefanie Meyer
Timothy Newton
Shane O'Neill
Patrick O'Sullivan
Tokimi Ota
Edward Ozimek
John Patkau
Patricia Patkau
Bill Pechet
Jan Raschke
Kathleen Robertson
Tom Robertson
Gordon Robinson

Chris Rowe
Lydia Schmansky
Christian Schulte
Martin Schwarzenbach
David Shone
Elizabeth Shotton
Martin Sigmund
Craig Simms
Kristine Solberg
Barry Stanton
Peter Sturzenegger
Steve Suchy
Nick Sully
Yong Sun
Peter Suter
Allan Teramura
Craig Thomas
Michael Thorpe
Tamara Ulisko
Bill Urich
Tom Van Driel
Mark Vaughn
Brian Wakelin
John Wall
Jacqueline Wang
Kevin Wharton
Peter Wood
Hale Youngblood
Jinyong Yum
Dohhee Zhong
Tom Zimmerman

Seabird Island School
Agassiz, British Columbia
1988–1991

Client: Seabird Island Band
Architect: Patkau Architects Inc.
Project Team: Gina Dhein, Greg Johnson, Andrew Larigakis, John Patkau, Patricia Patkau, Elizabeth Shotton, Tom Van Driel
Consultants: C. Y. Loh Associates Ltd., structural engineer; D. W. Thomson Consultants Ltd., mechanical/electrical engineer; Hanscomb Consultants Inc., costing consultant; Christopher Phillips & Associates, landscape architect; Novatec Consultants Inc., site development consultant
Contract Managers: Newhaven Projects Limited Partnership
Awards: Canadian Architect Award, 1989; Canadian Wood Council Honor Award, 1992; Governor General's Medal, 1992

Canadian Clay and Glass Gallery
Waterloo, Ontario
Winning Submission, National Design Competition, 1986
1988–1992

Client: City of Waterloo
Architect: Patkau Architects Inc.
Associate Architect: Mark Musselman McIntyre Combe Inc.
Project Team: Shelley Craig, Michael Cunningham, Tony Griffin, John Patkau, Patricia Patkau, Chris Rowe, Peter Suter
Consultants: C. Y. Loh Associates Ltd., structural engineer; Keen Engineering Co. Ltd., mechanical engineer; R. A. Duff & Associates Inc., electrical engineer; Hanscomb Consultants Inc., costing consultant
Contractor: Ball Construction Inc.
Awards: Canadian Architect Award, 1990; Governor General's Medal, 1997

Newton Library
Surrey, British Columbia
1990–1992

Client: Corporation of the District of Surrey
Architect: Patkau Architects Inc.
Project Team: Michael Cunningham, John Patkau, Patricia Patkau, David Shone, Peter Suter, Peter Wood
Consultants: C. Y. Loh Associates Ltd., structural engineer; D. W. Thomson Consultants Ltd., mechanical engineer; R. A. Duff & Associates Inc., electrical engineer; BTY Group, costing consultant; Brown Strachan Associates, acoustics consultant
Contractor: Farmer Construction Ltd.
Awards: Canadian Wood Council Merit, 1994; Governor General's Medal, 1994

Barnes House
Nanaimo, British Columbia
1991–1993

Client: David and Fran Barnes
Architect: Patkau Architects Inc.
Project Team: Timothy Newton, John Patkau, Patricia Patkau, David Shone, Tom Robertson
Consultants: Fast & Epp Structural Engineers, structural engineer
Contractor: R. W. (Bob) Wall Ltd.
Awards: Canadian Architect Award, 1992; Progressive Architecture Award, 1992; Architectural Record Award, 1996; Governor General's Medal, 1997

Strawberry Vale Elementary School
Victoria, British Columbia
1992–1995

Client: Greater Victoria School District
Architect: Patkau Architects Inc.
Project Team: Grace Cheung, Michael Cunningham, Michael Kothke, Timothy Newton, John Patkau, Patricia Patkau, David Shone, Peter Suter, Allan Teramura, John Wall, Jacqueline Wang
Consultants: C. Y. Loh Associates Ltd., structural engineer; D. W. Thomson Consultants Ltd., mechanical engineer; Reid Crowther & Partners Ltd., electrical engineer; Duncan & Associates Engineering Ltd., civil engineer; Thurber Engineering Ltd., geotechnical engineer; Moura Quayle/Lanark Consultants Ltd., landscape architect; Gage-Babcock & Associates, fire protection consultant; BTY Group, costing consultant; Barron Kennedy Lyzun & Associates Ltd., acoustics consultant; Environmental Research Group, University of British Columbia School of Architecture, materials consultant; Susan Morris Specifications, specifications consultant; Vaitkunas Design Inc., signage consultant
Contractor: JCR Construction
Awards: Canadian Architect Award, 1994; Progressive Architecture Award, 1995; Governor General's Medal, 2002

Shaw House
Vancouver, British Columbia
1995–2000

Client: John Shaw
Architect: Patkau Architects Inc.
Project Team: Michael Cunningham, Joanne Gates, John Patkau, Patricia Patkau, Peter Suter, Brian Wakelin
Consultants: Fast & Epp Structural Engineers, structural engineer
Contractor: Glover Co Ltd.
Awards: Record House Selection, 2002; Governor General's Medal, 2004; American Institute of Architects Honor Award, 2005

Agosta House
San Juan Island, Washington
1996–2000

Client: William and Karin Agosta
Architect: Patkau Architects Inc.
Project Team: John Patkau, Patricia Patkau, David Shone
Consultants: Fast & Epp Structural Engineers, structural engineer
Contractor: Ravenhill Construction Inc.
Awards: North American Wood Design Honor Award, 2002; Governor General's Medal, 2004; American Institute of Architects Honor Award, 2005

Nursing and Biomedical Sciences Building
University of Texas Houston Health Science Center,
Houston, Texas
Winning Submission, International Design
Competition, 1996

Client: University of Texas, Houston Health Science Center
Architect: Patkau Architects Inc.
Project Team: Tom Bessai, Michael Cunningham, Maria
Denegri, Joanne Gates, Julie LaFreneire, Timothy Newton,
John Patkau, Patricia Patkau, David Shone, Peter
Sturzenegger, Steve Suchy, Peter Suter, Tamara Ulisko,
Kevin Wharton
Consultants: Ove Arup + Partners California,
structural/mechanical/electrical engineer
Awards: Canadian Architect Award, 1998; Progressive
Architecture Citation, 1999

La Petite Maison du Weekend
1998–1989

Client: Wexner Center for the Arts
Architect: Patkau Architects Inc.
Project Team: Timothy Newton, John Patkau, Patricia
Patkau
Consultants: Fast & Epp Structural Engineers, structural
engineer
Contractor: Boelling Smith Design with Patkau Architects
Awards: North American Wood Design Awards Citation,
2001; Royal Architectural Institute of Canada Innovation
in Architecture Award of Excellence, 2001

Grande Bibliothèque du Québec
Montreal, Quebec
Winning Submission, International Design
Competition, 2000
2000–2005

Client: Bibliothèque nationale du Québec
Architect: Patkau/Croft Pelletier/Menkès Shooner
Dagenais Architectes Associés
Project Team: Laura Arpiainen, Vaughn Berg, Greg
Boothroyd, Stephan Chevalier, Judy Cheung, Michael
Cunningham, Dominique Dumais, Michael Elkan,
Samantha Hayes, Timothy Newton, Patrick O'Sullivan, John
Patkau, Patricia Patkau, Kathleen Robertson, David Shone,
Craig Simms, Kristine Solberg, Nick Sully, Peter Suter
Consultants: Gilles Guité Architecte, consulting architect;
Jodoin Lamarre Pratte et Associés Architectes,
architectural support; Regroupement Nicolet Chartrand
Knoll Limitée/Les Consultants Géniplus Inc., structural
engineer; Le Consortium Bouthillette, Pariseau & Associés
Inc./Groupe HBA Experts-Conseils Inc., mechanical/elec-
trical engineer; NBBJ, lighting consultant; Legault
Davidson, acoustics consultant; Scenoplus, theatre con-
sultants; KJA Inc., elevators consultant; Technorm Inc.,
code consultant; Scheme Consultants, landscape architect
Contractor: Hervé Pomerleau

Gleneagles Community Centre
West Vancouver, British Columbia
2000–2003

Client: Corporation of the District of West Vancouver
Architect: Patkau Architects Inc.
Project Team: Omer Arbel, Greg Boothroyd, Joanne Gates,
Samantha Hayes, Patrick O'Sullivan, John Patkau, Patricia
Patkau, David Shone, Craig Simms
Consultants: Vaughan Landscape Planning & Design,
landscape architect; Fast & Epp Structural Engineers,
structural engineer; Earth Tech Canada Inc., mechanical/
electrical engineer; Webster Engineering Ltd., civil
engineer; Gage-Babcock & Associates, code consultant;
Susan Morris Specifications, specifications consultant;
McSquared System Design Group, audiovisual consultant;
Gallop/Varley, signage consultant
Project Manager: Maurice J. Ouellette Consulting
Contractor: Country West Construction Ltd.

Winnipeg Centennial Library Addition
Winnipeg, Manitoba
Winning Submission, Design Competition, 2002
2002–2005

Client: City of Winnipeg Library Services
Architect: Patkau Architects Inc./LM Architectural Group
Project Team: Samantha Hayes, Maureen Kwong, Hector
Lo, Imke Maron, Tokimi Ota, John Patkau, Patricia Patkau,
Christian Schulte, Craig Simms, Yong Sun, Peter Suter
Consultants: Crosier Kilgour & Partners Ltd., structural
engineer; SMS Engineering Ltd., mechanical engineer;
MCW/AGE Consulting Professional Engineers, electrical
engineer; Hilderman Thomas Frank Cram Landscape
Architecture and Planning, landscape architect
Contractor: Manshield Construction Inc.
Awards: Canadian Architect Award of Excellence, 2004

Centre for Music, Art, and Design
University of Manitoba, Winnipeg, Manitoba
2002–ongoing

Client: University of Manitoba
Architect: Patkau Architects Inc./LM Architectural Group
Project Team: Greg Boothroyd, Wan Fa Guo, Hector Lo,
Stefanie Meyer, John Patkau, Patricia Patkau, Martin
Sigmund, Craig Simms, Hale Youngblood
Consultants: Crosier Kilgour & Partners Ltd., structural
engineer; SMS Engineering Ltd., mechanical engineer;
MCW/AGE Consulting Professional Engineers, electrical
engineer; Hilderman Thomas Frank Cram Landscape
Architecture and Planning, landscape architect; PCL
Constructors Canada Inc., costing consultant; Daniel Lyzun
& Associates, acoustics consultant; McSquared System
Design Group, audiovisual consultant
Awards: Canadian Architect Award of Excellence, 2005

Prototype Cottage
Lake of Bays, Ontario
2004

Client: Jack and Suzy Wadsworth
Architect: Patkau Architects Inc.
Project Team: Tina Becker, Oliver Birett, John Patkau,
Patricia Patkau, Craig Simms

Little House
West Vancouver, British Columbia
2004–ongoing

Client: Brian and Joan Lai
Architect: Patkau Architects Inc.
Project Team: Christoph Boeckeler, John Patkau, Patricia
Patkau, Craig Simms, Peter Suter
Consultants: EnNova Structural Engineers Inc.,
structural engineer
Awards: Canadian Architect Award of Excellence, 2005

New College House Student Residence
University of Pennsylvania, Philadelphia, Pennsylvania
2004

Client: University of Pennsylvania
Architect: Patkau Architects Inc.
Project Team: Tina Becker, Oliver Birett, Michael
Cunningham, Gregory Graemiger, Samantha Hayes, Juliane
Heinrich, Laura Killam, Hector Lo, Kayna Merchant, John
Patkau, Patricia Patkau, Craig Simms
Consultants: CVM Structural Engineers, structural engineer;
Arup, mechanical/electrical/plumbing engineer; Boles,
Smyth Associates Inc., civil engineer; Reed Hilderbrand
Associates Inc., landscape architect; Becker & Frondorf,
costing consultant; Gage-Babcock & Associates, code con-
sultant
Awards: Canadian Architect Award of Excellence, 2004

University Square
University of British Columbia, Vancouver, British Columbia
Competition Project, 2005

Client: University of British Columbia
Architect: Patkau Architects Inc.
Project Team: Tina Becker, Christoph Boeckeler, Greg
Boothroyd, Maureen Kwong, Michael Leckie, Hector Lo,
Kayna Merchant, Edward Ozimek, John Patkau, Patricia
Patkau, Craig Simms, Peter Suter, Jinyong Yum
Consultants: Keen Engineering Co. Ltd., mechanical/elec-
trical engineer; Fast & Epp Structural Engineers, structural
engineer; PWL Partnership Landscape Architects Inc.,
landscape architect; BTY Group, costing consultant